MW00711006

Driving the Back Road Home

Cover Design: Sally Johnson
Special Thanks to: Hannah Bissell and Teresa Mei Chuc

ISBN-13: 978-0-9907958-3-4
ISBN-10: 0990795837

Library of Congress Control Number: 2015932258

Shabda is the Sanskrit word for "sound, speech." Shabda is the sound current vibrating in all creation referred to as the Audible Life Stream, Inner Sound, and Word. Founded in June 2011 by Teresa Mei Chuc, Shabda Press' mission is to bring forth the luminous words and sounds of new, emerging, and established voices.

Published by Shabda Press
Pasadena, CA 91107
www.shabdapress.com

Acknowledgements: Poems in this book were originally published in the following magazines and literary journals:

American Literary Arts Review, Atlanta Review, Birmingham Poetry Review, Calliope, Chiron Review, Concho River Review, Contraposition, Coyote's Journal, Cutbank, Descant, Drumlummon Views, Hubbub, Huerfano, ICON, Inkwell, The Iowa Review, Ithica Lit, Limestone, Mas Tequila Review, Miramar, Negative Capability, Oxford Magazine, Pacific Review, Pinyon Review, Poem, Poet Lore, Poetry Now, Pudding, Puerto del Sol, Rattle, Red Fez, River Sedge, Rockhurst Review, South Coast Poetry Journal, Steam Ticket, Trestle Creek Review, Two Cities Review, Weber Studies, White Pelican Review, and *Wilderness Poetry Review.*

Created, produced, and designed in the United States.
Printed in the United States.

Driving the Back Road Home

poems by

Lowell Jaeger

Shabda Press
Pasadena, CA 91107

Driving the Back Road Home

I. This We Do for Love

II. Lucky Us

III. This Day and Age

IV. Accidentally Still Blue

I. This We Do for Love

And here we are in the middle, holding it all together,
not even shaking.

— William Stafford

I don't regret how much I love,
and I avoid those who repent their passions.

— Rumi

scout camp

sure we dug latrines
laced lanyards
learned to keep food cool in a dirt pit
baked mock strudel
in tinfoil ovens
the heat carefully kept in check
by nudging and fanning glowing embers

and learned
— when the adults turned away —
to share a single purloined stogie
our green faces greener
in the smoke-filled moonlight
our bristled crewcuts huddled
over one failing pocketlight
spotlighting girlie mags
page after page

i'd swear a scout's oath
i heard the trees listening
and woke in the mist before sunrise
to wander far as the trail would wind

as fiddleheads unfolded
and pines pollinated pines

and the earth held my steps steady
and the sky gave me room to climb

wings

not everything exists yet
a butterfly told me
through mason glass
untwisting me

to lift the lid
watch him fly
watch tides of prairie grass
bending to accord
a sun-glittered meadow's
flitting design . . .

i was ten that summer
hundreds died i had no use for

i remember flowers
spreading rumors about me
dragonflies eavesdropping on my fishpole
bluegills strung like smuggled jewels
hooked on drowning mayflies

i used to walk home
down long graveled roads
broken wings
dancing on my battered earth

singing in tongues

grandma's geraniums

grandma's geraniums
in clusters of terracotta pots
frothing white minerals
leeching through clay

and legions more
bounding pathways she trod
back and forth across the meadow

past crippled sheds and greenhouses
leaning toward collapse

her steps crisp as dried leaves
her dark eyes cold
as buckets of rain
lifted from the cistern

she'd flinch from almost touching
grandchildren trailing too near
mewling at her apron strings
for cookies and treats

she'd shoo us away
brushing past us
as if fleeing a plague of gnats . . .

june's booming downpour
soaking her smock
as she cradled her geraniums to safety
where we sheltered in the barn
and shivered amidst a flood

of blossoms bursting red

children after school

one kicks a half-deflated
beach ball
mock hacky-sack
solitaire

till another and others
call out from windows
to come play

amidst parked cars
rutted asphalt
ragged skies

birds huddle
on the powerlines
bickering like kids

chattering
some bittersweet need
to flock

and fly

after the class picnic

she worried about the barbed wire
how she might tear her dress
a sunflower print her mom's hands
had snipped and stitched
to mark a daughter's passage
eighth-grade's last day

one strand of barbs
i boot-heeled low in the weeds
and lifted another skyward
to open our way

along the cow path
across the pasture
to climb the rocky outcrop
balanced over frothing torrents
of crash and spray

give me your hand i said
though when she reached
my chest forgot
how the air should flow

she'd stepped through the fence safely
eyes keen
with a kindling glow . . .

her hand in mine
and she wouldn't let go

haunted

floats room to room like a ghost
said my mother
meaning me

what's wrong she'd ask
and i couldn't name it
just wanted to be alone
didn't know why

wanted to turn my collar up
walk in the rain

or nights when the clouds opened
wanted to sit at the window
stare at the starlit sky

midsummer's dream

outside the pavilion
a classmate
stubbed a toe
lost a flipflop . . .

i carried her on my shoulders
her tan thighs
locked around my neck

dark streets
warm night
home to her mother's house

kneeled at the front porch
to let her stand again
plant a quick peck on my cheek

watched her
hobble up the steps
and through the screen door

walked home alone
that's all
end of story

ambled the long way home
just me and the stars
aching
so wondrous

this extraordinary
unfolding

any ordinary day

old red bridge

she led me past barricades
closed road sign
onto boards and rusted steel
her hand in my hand
ice-blue waters beneath us
a roiling flow

recalling limbs she'd climbed
as a kid perched in cottonwoods
leaning over the cutbank
or stones smoothed in currents
her bare feet had come to know

with fistfuls of mane
she'd thrown her arms around the neck
of an unsteady stallion spooked
into sprinting
the bridge's entire suspended span

but she'd held on she said
like this
right here right now

and she was holding me
showing me how

how

how do skin-helmeted mushrooms
push their heads through my driveway's
rubbled hardpack

how do hummingbirds buzz
north from buenos aires to sip
my garden's nectars half a planet away

how do columbine lupine dog-vine
and all their green kind
kindle an ember through sub-zero sleep

how do invisible threads tether
our lonesome rock as we race
through vast deserts of black space

how does it come to pass
lightning strikes one place
and not another nearby

and what are the odds of you and i
colliding face to face
how impossible to guess

that first night i asked
how i'd braced for a likely no
and you said yes

this we do for love

had to roll the window open partway
clear a narrow porthole
in the frosted windshield
to follow how the road twisted
fishtailing through snow
monotonous miles of corn stubble
half a night's drive

in a battered vee-dub bus
cobbled with baling wire
bad shocks and bald tires
slapping myself to keep awake
when the radio stuttered and quit
crooning my own reckless lonesome ballads
my lovesick obsessions

and she . . .
ecstatic with crazy worry
pacing her rented rooms
listening to storm broadcasts
listening to the clock
candles lit and flickering
table set with cheese and soup
and bread and wine

kept a chair close against the window
waiting breathless
counting headlights passing in the streets below
praying for mine

rainy afternoon

we lay with our legs entwined
breath to breath
mattress on the floor
candle-nub sputtering
on the nightstand

windows crying cold rain

our ghosts of persistent forebodings
we couldn't fend off
for long in the troubled face
of imminent consequence
headed our way . . .

but these hours we held onto each other
side by side
as the candle flickered
as traffic on the iced streets below
passed and repeated

clung to this one afternoon
as the windows welled up with rain

and secretly
i pocketed
forever the locket of her face

nuzzled to my ear

the buoy

crowds flowing along the walkway
your face in a sea of faces
bobbing

and the bell in your heart still chimes

quarrel

i’m sorry to the bone
whatever i said or failed to say
when the woman i lay beside
turned away

can’t sleep can’t think
with my heartbeat racing

what else to do
but dress in the dark
step outside to breathe
the shock of sub-zero midnight

what else to do
but hike the abandoned logging road
into waiting hillsides of calm

stand in a meadow
winded

breaths huffing
small prayers
skyward

after she'd moved out

i hustle across campus as the bell tower chimes
count the hours hammered
muddled meanwhile between
the rock of her goodbye and the hard place
of her never coming back

women i barely know
offer sympathetic looks
pat my hand
as a mother might comfort a child

one leaves a warm sack breakfast on my desk
her laced signature attached

cards of fondest wishes
bubble up with chocolate kisses
while others pray lots pray
i'm shocked so many believe
they might part the heavens a crack
on my behalf

as i reach into the sack to nibble a roll
so warm so sweet

as the bell tower gongs another hour passed
as i tally echoing chimes but lose track
swallow hard
late for my next class

woodcutter's breakdown

the saw choked when its chain snagged
having torn a tall larch
halfway to the core

i'd guessed which direction wrong
this giant
would give way

the cut closed
i fell backwards
scrambled clear
and woke that instant
cowed on the forest floor
the saw's moan floating skyward

so much noise i'd made
to muffle over losing you
so much work to be done
i'd refused to grieve

the saw smoldered
stuck fast in wood that bit back

clouds puffed and floated past

i felt the eyes of the forest on me
the listening of a thousand trees

and cried like a man cries
silently
where no one sees

world lit

we were discussing the protagonist
his heart
overrun with bitterness

a long silence
washed across the classroom
as each of us felt his pulse quicken

and i confessed i'd been betrayed
in love recently
remembered shutting the alarm off
months of mornings
wanting to pull the blankets over my head

i was sorry the instant i'd spoken
but tumbled forward asking
what was it
so unnerved me

someone nodded
they'd felt the same
then each pair of eyes in turn
lit with recognition

the chill of waking from a dream
the daily gut ache of dashed expectations
and like our protagonist
the rueful habit of loving a difficult world
though it seldom loves us back

motel six lament

a reprinted landscape
bolted against cinderblock
motel walls

this farm-scape steaming
with prairie's august dragon blast
over unbounded blossoms
and meadows of tall grass

through which a foolish man runs
arms flapping
as if in flight
as if the sun flares so buoyantly
he could be lifted

and held
in the great wide-open of your small palm

where my heart winged skyward
that picnic afternoon
a week before graduation
a thousand miles ago

when we drove panoramic back roads
windows open

your eyes smiling like a plashing stream
the lilt of your laughter
like crickets hid in the cattails
like bees euphoric in the corn

blink of an eye ago

seems like the blink of an eye ago
she ventured small steps
trembling up the pathway
in wedding lace and flowers
past well-wishers
still a girl on her father's arm

but as to the exact words
or precise sequence of ceremony
forgive me i'm blank
between when she locked her gaze
bravely to mine
and clamorous applause
as we fumbled the rings
and kissed a bit shyly

then to wake unsuspectingly
years forward skin-to-skin
beneath thick quilts
in this blazing miraculous
heart-thumping tender
persistent blissful urge

as again her lids flicker open
with a glint of mischief
dawning in the half-dark
wordlessly
and i press my face close
smiling my reply

wishing on a white horse

my wife and i risk death
driving home over ice and snow
late morning new year's day

unrelenting sun on shifting drifts
slicing my optic nerve
and the only shades i own
left behind in some damn saloon

i'm wishing on a white horse
sheltered in a scatter of rocks
my wish steaming with the stallion's breath
heavenward

it's my grandfather's lucky benediction
a white horse
out of nowhere like this one
gracing a bedeviled vista . . .

wish i hadn't snapped at her
when she'd questioned the roads i'd chosen

wish we could love each other
better than we do

she's asleep now
a moment ago complaining
her head throbbed

half-accusing me
of bumping the worst ruts on purpose

happy

she'd dashed her invitation
on a postcard aerial view
of idaho's wild
flowering meadows

her newfound brothers and sisters
a communal farm
happy happy happy
like heaven she said

i imagined waltzing with fairybells
woven in my hair
singing kumbaya till my jaw ached
smiling all day long

considered a diet of black beans
sprouts and soy burgers
my flatulent comrades and i
lined up outside the outhouse door

and though i was lonely at the time
i was mostly attracted by the thought
of wandering solo in those meadows
contented

without need
to wriggle myself loose
from twelve doe-eyed sisters
tugging at my tie-dye lovingly

the tease

en route to the family farmstead
i think of my sister
how she'd fallen into obsession
with planting and harvesting

she'd had a boyfriend once
he'd called her ladybug
his little chickpea
his squash blossom

then vanished like a dirt-devil
evaporates mid-swirl

overnight she'd transformed
acres of loveless scrub
into neat little rows
of beets and potatoes and beans

having married
her faithful rake and spade

her fair-skinned face
now tanned and leathered
her hands positively
tattooed green

what about love

talking about
what's happiness
what's worth living for
and each of us
at the campfire

takes his turn one says
climbing to the summit
one says ski racing one says
the airplane he's saving to buy. . .

the last after a pause says
his dog and we think it's a joke
hey he says hey
that dog needs me
like i need to be needed
he looks around
all of us laughing
seriously he says
dead serious

so we go back to sipping beers
a gang of single guys
weekend in the woods
each of us
            puzzling
about being needed
about love
none of us mentions love

and the night falls
silent
          some of us
looking to the stars

some of us
staring at the flames

II. Lucky Us

Wake up! scolds the raven sailing off
over the canyon. Wake up! Wake up! Wake up!

– Steve Kowit

Let the beauty we love be what we do.
There are hundreds of ways to kneel and kiss the ground.

– Rumi

house plant

someone snuffed his butt
in your pot
and you've forborn this indignity
alone
while i've read under lamplight
beside you nightly

and absent-mindedly plucked
a small leaf
folded it and rolled it
between my thumb and index finger
and held it to my nose

till my book fell shut

where i'd been contemplating
the nobility of human compassion
or the tragedy
of a lack thereof . . . .

forgive me
we've inhabited these same walls
for how long

and i don't even know your name

needs to be done

i cradle her weight in my coat sleeves
stumbling over uncertain footholds of crusted snow
across brambles and up steep hillsides
toward a clearing i sometimes go
to look out over the lake in the valley below

she's dripping shit on my cuffs and boots

i mess up the lord's prayer in a mumble
when i dig to unearth it and the psalms
are only shards of song but i land on
good old do unto others
do as you would
have them do to you no question but

when the sun rises someday i can't
eat can't stop pissing on the carpet
can't walk without listing toward a fall . . .

lift me with considerate pity to a grand
last view let it be one special someone
who looks me in the eye
says goodbye and

triggers a merciful blast to kingdom come

snow blind

lost my way snowshoeing
near the summit
in a confusion of iridescent sky
and a trillion watts of glacial sunshine
till horizons glared
blurred
washed black

tied a bandana blindfold
stood dumbstruck
impatient
prayed light come back come back

glimpsed how each of us survives
stumbling with his eyes closed
delivered headlong
before the world comes clear

sweat like an unborn infant
trembling
a panicked drumbeat in my ear

alone

don’t ask the stars
stars ask nothing back

listen
your campfire’s lick and snap

the splash and ripple
of river pulsing past

inhale the sage

mumble over fallen logs
heaps of rot and crumble

mimic the shushing
breathing pine

or rave and squawk
then tongue the flutter of black
feathers

lifting lifting

even the loam breathes

leonard youngbear says
in the old days there was no such thing
as trash
native camps left ashes only
or bones bits of hide feathers
mounds of buffalo dung

what dogs didn't eat
coyotes did
or wind snow rain
beneath trees and prairie grass
everything from the earth
returned

human life too leonard says
should be like that . . .

says don't please don't
box him in a casket
when it's time
it's time

his carcass melts into the wild he says
where a small swallow of him
will struggle upstream
in a rainbow's fantail

while a morsel of his putrid flesh
strengthens the wings of a fledgling
straining to fly

lucky us

along the goat path
winding who-knows-where
our foursome
resting on a rock ledge
chewing trail mix
talking about luck
who's lucky
who's not

look oh look
one of us points

a wolverine loping
through gnarled dwarf conifers
sniffing like a hound
toward his next meal

in silence we witness
this chance of a lifetime
lucky us
watching him flow
as if he's swimming
through undulating meadows
of yellow lilies
and crystalline rivulets
of glacial alpine streams

on the trail to the world's largest doug fir

we've shed zippered insulated comforts
climbed out of our tent
naked
into damp coastal fog so thick
we can't find topmost boughs
where these giant firs breathe

both of us hushed
stepping barefoot careful
over rocks and roots and rubble
up our short path
to the icy dribble of mountain stream

then bending to splash and bathe
waking the hairs on our arms
our bodies goose-bumped
smiling mute
shivering in the flow

while the wilderness surrounding us listens
knowing what can't be said
knowing all there is to know

we can live together this far apart

at the summit
clouds are nesting
in damp meadows

a brief sun burns an opening
to floodlight
a scant hundred yards downwind
a bear
craning his nose
ears forward

i back away
he steps back too
both of us facing the other
and limits of common ground

think about bears
who have traversed acres i call my own
to feed in orchards
along the lakeshore
hunted back into the hills
harried by traffic and barking dogs

consider how i've invaded his retreat
how my human footprint
increases relentlessly

my boot heels along the trail home
kicking rocks loose
echoing down the mountainside

small ears in the underbrush
listening

each of my footfalls
sounding alarm

slaughter

my son ranks a platoon
of plastic infantrymen
and mows them down
with a spray of pretend bullets
hissed from his teeth

prods a lone survivor
at rubber knife point
to climb a couch cushion
and plunges him to cruel demise
face-first in the dog dish

i'm under the eaves
napalming bees
after i'd dusted
an impersonal end of everything
to an anthill metropolis

while the cat corners a vole
and a screaming jay swoops to feed
on a swallowtail flitting past

the glittered disembodied wings
floating earthward

blissfully detached

coyote pups

cop-car siren
wailing such a high pitch
my little dog yips a string
of painful yowls
                    to my surprise

up the hill behind our home
inside acres of trees and bramble
roars a chorus of coyote pups
joining my shih-tzu's plaintive song

i hold the dog's leash
taut
pause in aspen's rippled shade
after the cop-car's passing

picture the pups' borough
a bed of moss and fern nestled
in gnarled roots of tall pine
where mama cuffs her brood to shush

and like an awakening sleepwalker
i'm wide-eyed suddenly
apprehending for the first time
the din of squirrel chitters and whistling birds

claws scuttling in the underbrush
dark wings wuff-wuffing through
treetops where

even the leaves
seem to be mumbling something

shoots of something green

shoots of something green
leaking through blistered pavement
at the edge of my driveway

i spray herbicides
seal the upheavals
with two coats of hot tar

by next thaw
new fractures new
tangles of thorny vines

this morning i slither
into crawl space beneath my floors
cower like a man in a cave
to inspect rotted footings and supports

earth's persistent breath
fanning
dust and rubble

coaxing pale leafless runners
bursting through clods
worming toward hairline faults

in the broken resolve
of my concrete foundation

dust to dust

dust to dust
i've heard them say
part of us
just blown away

by the river i sit
watch it fall
can't believe
dust is all

what about the water part
sweat and piss
my bloody heart

drop by drop
with ocean tides
my body's currents ride

snow-melt trickles
in each vein
this earthen vessel
carries rain

scatology

i drop my drawers
and lean back
over a fallen jack pine

brace my elbows
on my knees

bears do it
birds and squirrels
even slugs
gnats
aphids too

easy to spot elk and deer doo
complex record of just who
passed by
and when

i stand
zip and then
study my scat-print
stuff i'm stuffed with
earth to earth

mud
of our maker's design

it was

hardly a grease stain
near the graveled roadside
and before that

a weather-torn canvas tarp
over scraps of spine
and before that

bones licked bright as moonlight
chewed to the marrow
and before that

wild dogs feasting on entrails
magpies reaming eye sockets
and before that

a bloated stink of flies
four shaggy hocks unshod hooves
and before that

she lifted the drudge
of my daily drive
from home and back

this pinto mare grazing
in the boulder-strewn foothills
sun glazing her dappled flanks

breezes combing her long white mane

this tomato

its juices
drip from my chin

i potted the seed
watched it begin

morning to morning
watched it transform

sheltered the blossom
from cold from storm

added soil and sunshine
and rain

fruit on my tongue
no life is plain . . .

just taste it
don't explain

the owl

a small quake
up and down my spine
told me he was there

even before i'd turned
to find him perched
in a broken cottonwood

watching over me
where i stood in the barnyard
alone i'd thought

after pedaling back roads
of rutted gravel
sweat-soaked sunburned miles

----

he'd been puzzling my mumble
as i searched where the brambles
had overtaken collapsed
sheds and corrals

his head turned sidewise
one eye then another
blinking

----

the branch beneath him
snapping clean and falling
when his wings spread wide

gliding till i'd lost him
in the sun's radiant
glare

----

the shattered branch
tumbling over itself
floating feather-like
earthward

stabbing in the dust
peppering my shadow
with clods and debris

----

i'd uncovered the pump handle
and replenished
my canteen

swallowed long pulls
of rust-water
bled cold from bedrock

glad
in the loneliness of my bones
as a man can ever be

as i mounted and pedaled onward
the owl
staying with me

from someplace unseen

Part III. This Day and Age

There are books in which the footnotes or comments scrawled by some reader's hand in the margins are more interesting than the text. The world is one of these books.

— Santayana

showgirl

asks me for a light
— her smoke break between shows —
stands telling me
there's a crash coming
no power no gas
she says
your dollars won't be worth shit

she's a confused conspiracy
of ridiculous contradiction
clad in star-spangled thong bikini
sequined platform heels
feathered bejeweled headdress
aztec goddess casino queen

my daughter's age maybe less
exposed and disclosing
her dream to seclude herself she says
in a wild-country log-wall hideout
with a trout stream undulating nearby
beds of garden veggies
and tittering meadow-fed hens . . .

wants to live like who she is she says
dance or not dance as she chooses
outside police-state satellite surveillance
loosed from the attentions of strangers
beyond range of any one of several
crazy ex-boyfriends out on parole

how money changes hands

on the casino floor
you can squander an hour in line
greedy for your turn to lock yourself
in a tiny glass booth

where a powerful fan
flutters paper currency
like bees like bats

sixty seconds to stand
and grab
swirling storms
of cash

your arms flailing
a frenzied spectacle

emerging with a fistful of glee
when the doors whoosh open

and you're mister mega-bucks
riding his adrenaline rush
flagging a cocktail waitress
coaxing her smile

here ya go hon
your entire prize of three dollars
proffered
like a magnanimous tycoon

though still a bit shaken
a bit dumbfounded

how she reaches
eagerly
and gladly

takes it

all this

consider please blood of my blood
all this shopping and gathering all this
enterprise and ownership all this
money changing
hands

these racks and racks
miles of aisles
stacks and stacks

today's double-stuffed over-stuffed
cash and carry
steal-of-a-deal holiday specials

(while cold winds squall
through foreclosed hollows
of our impoverished hearts)

as we dally in line
mindlessly minding our carts
and carts and carts
of precious ridiculous
hilarious bling

in the muffled mad muzak
of ka-ching ka-ching ka-ching

i'm no fun to take shopping

sidelined on a plastic bench
in the mall
while the wife and kids
kill another credit card

i think about the hours exhausted
blood-hounding a particular pair of shoes
and shirt to match that sweater on sale
tote-bagged home last week

think about how markets
target us
with shotgun enticements
of holiday discount come-ons

think about fleets of shopping carts encumbered
dumpsters and landfills swamped with bilge
garages boggy with yard-sale flotsam
lodged where the car should park

think about our own abode
the treasures we've stashed
clutter we haven't heart to part with

opulent tons of twaddle
till drawers can't open
till pantry shelves sag and stagger
till closet doors won't fold closed

shopper's creed

bless us excitable monkeys
cavorting in your mall
greedy for monkey grub

offer us merchandise on sale
whether we need it or not
and bedazzle us with neon sheen

lead us not to resist instant credit
but deliver us from common sense
and bestow us with bewildering debt

for thine is the glittered and golden
which maketh us jump up and down
for irresistible holiday discounts

and monthly installment plans for all
every monkey's tote bag laden
with manufactured disposal nonsense

guaranteed landfill dreck
which chaineth us to ledgers and wages
forever indentured more

performance evaluation

three grey suits making lunch
of one young trainee
table next to mine

she nods like a bobble-head
sits upright wide-eyed
yes yes of course yes

syllables of nothing
and everything her three superiors
have come to hear

this corporate firing squad
in service to the high command
the bottom line

teacup in her hand trembling
smiling a barbed wire boundary
between business as it is
and the career she'd hope it might be

between decorum and devastation
between compliance and rage

big-city girl

she's pulled to the roadside
to use her cell phone
just answer a call
that's all
just answer an ordinary call
from a friend
and it's downright annoying
she says
in a small town like this
all these people
so concerned
they slow down
they stop
they ask
are you okay
are you okay

fine she says
yes she says
i'm fine
just talking on the phone

really they ask
and squint suspiciously
really they ask
and she says really
and they say
you're sure
and she says i'm sure
and they say you're sure you're sure
and she says
i'm fine
i'm okay
i'm sure
really sure
really

so easy

no need to bust a knuckle chipping flints
chew-soften sinew
belly-crawl half naked
through thistles and cinders

now meats are shrink-wrapped
bloodless
stacked in my cart

i glide
toward the checkout
over polished vinyl
the cashier sacking
prepackaged sustenance
for the suburban cave

no need for brewed pigments
to paint for posterity
millenniums forward
how I feed the clan

how we sup so leisurely
afterwards rest easy
stare at the ceiling
reach for a ballpoint pen
open this notebook

jot this down

charity

i’d already surrendered
one hard-earned twenty
having been duped
by this teary-eyed con
bantamweight beggar
tussling at my coat sleeve
moaning his woeful opus

how did we signal so loudly
our small town lack
of defenses to fend him back
ascending to street level
spilled from the metro underground
amidst a confounding noon-hour crush
into blinding daylight glare

while savvy locals
shrugged and smirked
said tell him to fuck off

as he snatched my cash
pressed his goat breath closer
promised he’d repay
pledged he’d repay
crossed himself and doubled his fervor
plying for more

thought it would be easy

big metal desk with my name
county social services
college junior summer job
paid just to listen
to people's grievances
decide who's qualified
what type of support

learned to cradle my coffee cup
both palms
like an ember to carry
one interview into the next
and next

opened file drawers
selected appropriate forms
sent her across the hall to room 3b
or him to 2c or her to 4d
upstairs to the attorneys
downstairs to the cops

wished i could unlatch a window

sort of twisted me
watching time crawl

faces voices ages changed
if anything changed

at all

why we feel alone

physicists calculate
matter is mostly not

mostly a lot of emptiness
surrounding atoms

galaxies of vast
invisible loneliness

picture the night sky
awash with stars

each light adrift
in sweeping spaces between

or these masses of passing flesh
shoulder to shoulder

milling in the streets
clusters of nothingness

swimming in the illusion
of intimate proximity

contemporary art

don't shake your head
and walk away don't
throw up your hands

this muddle of oddball clutter
these walls dripping graffiti
these marbled halls echoing our talk

it's just what it is
we say because it's not
what it's not

this wondrous ordinary
everyday strange
this weird tripping vertigo

is what we wake up with
the familiarly outlandish
asking us to look

in the mirror
asking us
what the hell is it

what's it all about

why print books

why print books he said
who needs books these days
everything's on the web

well i wouldn't know i said
i still enjoy turning pages
in a chair by the fire

still window-shop mainstreet
still relish a big screen matinee
buttered popcorn jujubes and milk duds

still sit and think about how
all last century carriages went horseless
and horses thank god are not extinct

still long for real letters in the post
the effort of someone's penmanship
the dear and sincerely yours

just bought a case of new and improved
better than edison lightbulbs
mega kilowatt compact florescent

and still i'd rather light candles
strike sparks with someone i love
in near dark face-to-face

backcountry mercantile

park in weeds and wild blossoms
now that miles of washboard gravel
ruts and potholes
have slowed you to stopping

open the merc's screen door
and let it bang behind you

let
your eyes breathe
the sweet yeasty rising
of muffins plumped just right

sit and savor
a steaming wake-up mug
of burn-your-datebook coffee

munch sell-the-condo trailmix brownies
thick with oats
enough to seed an acre

let the rest of the world keep it straight

and smile back at the aproned matron
tending her ovens
dipping her shoulders and hips
playing her long hair easy
side to side

a dance
like you wish you knew how

custer

one day custer
comes knocking

chief he says
suppose i let you in on my little secret

puts his arm around me
talks his best indian-talk
many moons
heap big
that sort of thing

his breath smells
like he's been munching buffalo chips

here's my card
he says
send me the old smoke signal
when you're ready to sell

prairie paradise
the card says
one-acre building sites

he's an old man in a leisure suit
very tan
thick gold chain around his neck

he's lost all his hair
but i'm dead sure

it's still george

people are mostly the same

this singular gent
slants his hat in a dashing manner
hammering his quick steps
erect and imperious
as if he owns the pavement beneath him

as if he isn't dogged
same as we are hounded by self-doubt
worries aches and pains

still . . . he's an enlightening surprise
in the way he stoops and retrieves a lucky penny
hints he's a familiar mix
of hidden vexations

the way he wipes it on his sleeve
cleans it of grime
the way he leans at the bridge rail
listening
to the coin's splash and ripple

wishing his wish
eyes closed

voices

voices float
from a public phone
hung in the hallway

breathing themselves under my door

don’t lie to me she says
then a brittle silence
just don’t lie

or the young shoe salesman
i’ve changed he pleads
why can’t i come home

now and again someone from the outside
dials and the phone jingles alone

just yesterday
a man confessed to his best girl
how the taxi business wore him thin
everybody’s got someplace to go he said
i miss you

and it hurt
how his whisper reached up at the closing
not like he had something to tell
love you he said

sort of a question

what we do

let's tell it with no slant
we did what we did
we'd taunt him chase him for blocks
like a pack of jackals
toying with defenseless prey

he'd sweat and blush
and stutter l-l-l-leave me alone
turn and flee
hips swishing like a girl

wish i could shrug it off
what we did we did
mostly i followed mostly did nothing
just watched like i wasn't there

we were high school jocks
and he was a grown man
i did nothing
broad daylight in plain sight

while mainstreet merchants
cops and shoppers
looked away

ruin

(Hamburg, Germany)

this lone surviving pocked gothic spire
its fractured buttresses clinging
to a single stone wall scorched black

teeth of the priest
bones of the congregation

mounds of rubble and ash
where the heat of the blast
flashed beneath our wings

like a distant star incidentally blinking

air show

should be easy to join this contagious thrill
this holiday spectacle
the mass of us jostling for best views
backpacked with provisions to last the day

applauding and trembling in awe
at these glossed blue and gold war machines'
sky ballet
these praiseworthy mechanical marvels . . .

but i'm queasy when i stretch to grasp
the hand commanding the guns the bombs
these f-somethings' wings
built to shatter unsheltered heads in the crosshairs

these angels catching us
enraptured
the boom and growl of the burn
trailing after

casualties

when will the soldiers come
she asks as we glide
on the porch swing near dark

she's seen something frightening on tv
whimpers and shakes
when she should be sleeping

i ask the first stars
to salvage this child's unsullied smile

where has it gone

i bundle her in thick quilts
and pull her near
till her lids flutter closed

change

the more things change
the bumper-sticker proclaims
the more they stay the same

what doesn't change
is all the talk about change
some favor it some fear it

some contriving we should die for it
countrymen conscripted
our collective blood spilling forth

like a burble of water weeps
high up the mountainside
gathers and falls

never the same river twice
we like to say but the river
doesn't say it and the soldier

weary on the riverbank stares
at the flow and knows
what he doesn't know

i own a small understanding

of this machine's
combustion
under extreme pressure
same way you build a bomb

devilry to do with torque specs
with gaskets guaranteed
will someday blow

with trusting rubber treads
to hold the road
except when they don't

a mass of steel and glass
crash-tested

damages reckoned
on the dummy inside
who apprehends no more
than what i know

as i wave my goodbye
strap myself in

and go

this day and age

1)

the wreck that t-boned
dad's buick out-of-the-blue
rammed through a red light

i was a kid in the back seat
crying and i'd re-live
red lights in dreams for years

the impact
the bang the crunch
lodged a cringe in the drum
of my ears

and wakes me still
nights far-off boxcars are coupling . . .

their shudder and buckle and slam

2)

a screaming stampede
fled the mall
– said tonight's news –

affrighted by an echoing boom

could have been a gunshot
was our first thought
said a man and a woman
embracing having escaped
to the streets in tears

no the newsman says
only a toppled display of glass
crashing
an accident

bystanders nod empathetically
who can be certain
others say
well . . . with the world what it is now . . .
this unpredictable day and age

Part IV. Accidentally Still Blue

I too live where there are no roads,
in the mist that turns most people back.

– Rilke

Just being there is a career.

—William Stafford

flying a poem

i’m up in the turbulence
watching out the window
praying the wings are bolted

and on the ground below
i’m staring upward and confused
as i fly past

squirrel

truly i cursed you
and your chattering kin
for burrowing under my decks
for chewing holes in the insulation
for trashing the pump house
with pinecones and debris

though when i found your entrails
fresh on the highway
in front of our driveway
near the mailbox
i paused to study you

your little beaver-teeth broken
your ears tufted black
toes and claws
the whole of your grasp
less than my thumbprint

your tail blood-crusted
as cars and trucks whooshed by

a few fine strands of fluff
lifting

motel

woman sobbing in the room
across the hall from mine

past midnight says the clock
tocking toward its morning alarm

i'm contemplating the ceiling
owl-eyed in the dark

a man's drunken voice rumbles
his volley of pinched curses

while the woman lets flow her wash
of low continuous moans

and i hold tight to a faraway siren
on a mission toward someone's call

imagine the ambulance like a speedboat
jetting through torrents of human turbulence

the driver mumbling at the controls
his face paled dash-light green

another long night of rescue
his weary practiced god-like calm

in a crossroads bar last night

two-steppers holding their partners close
shouting in each other's ears
above the band's booming brass

while bug-eyed whiskered fish hover
against the glass of their tank along one wall
straining to focus
the waterless world
murkier than their own

as pearl-buttoned cowgirls
shimmer like neon satin mermaids
laugh and crumble fish food in their palms
sprinkling crumbs
teasing the ancient lunkers upward
exclaiming look look
look at the size of that one

fish fighting for the bait gladly
roiling in a green sea-splash ballet
folding themselves into the action
like a nest of writhing snakes
like the rest of us
hungry for love

simple as that

if we owned a couple of rackets
and no net
we simply slapped the birdie back and forth
and could have worked it out
made a game of it
counting the volleys
toward better
and better scores
simple as that

but jeez we squabbled
like snakes and weasels
my brother and i
wasted whole afternoons
insisting on winners and losers
spitting insults
barbed like poison darts
arguing a disputed line-shot
foul or not

could come to blows
headlocks and sucker punches

could break records decades later
for months without contact
grown men habitually contending
feuding
like kids in a sandlot

simple as that

toothache

he's masked and gloved for protection
jabs my gums with his pain-killer
my neck wedged
between pads at the head of his chair
so that i stare heavenward
at italian alps papered on the ceiling

where i stroll in my fog of nitrous
head-phoned harp strings
amidst halcyon toothy crags
slopes of daisies blathering

till i glimpse the glinting edge
of his blade as he wipes bloody slime
across the bib on my chest
his rubber fingers smeared with goo

outside i weave toward my car in the lot
my tongue a cud of jerky
the bill despite its weighty sum
flags in the breeze
as nerves pulse and plug themselves
back into my circuits

and my wife drives me homeward
gravel crunching beneath our tread
past eroded pastures
where fractured boulders
ache like molars splitting in my head

referral to a specialist

tomorrow i'll stand exposed
to dr x's full inspection
sores on my face and back

where i'd blistered summers ago
shoulders and chest
nose peeled raw
shirtless barefoot miles
of boyhood graveled back roads

contemplating stars tonight
wishing for an incantation
to save my cancerous skin

while galaxies churn like grindstones
even suns blink and extinguish

and the gods who ignite us

let us burn

long black cadillac hearse

driver cadaverously pale
shimmering suit and tie
groomed for a public cruise

light goes green
my heart's racing
can't outpace him

next light i fake a turn
thank god
he doesn't follow

spend a creepy part of the day
whistling like i don't care
mocking
silly old superstitious me

worse than black cats
have crossed my path
and i'd never sweat
continuing where i'd intended

but this hearse deviled me to shivers
my face mirrored back
in the driver's silvered lenses . . .

i navigate a slow shortcut home
fasten my seatbelt
look both ways

accidentally still blue

three men with chainsaws
on a hillside overlooking
a busy highway below
drop a diseased giant
doug fir in front of my home
bending to the task
of sectioning the trunk
into rounds
like fat slices of salami

one round breaks free
crashes through brush downhill
slams into the ditch
leaps across both lanes
and rumbles on like a mad rhino
in a dust cloud of distant sage

the men stand and stare
jesus christ one says
a motorcycle whizzes past unsuspectingly
the rider's head bowed low

then a school bus and lumbering
tandem trailer semi load of timbers

jesus the one says again
the other mops his brow
the other inhales a sigh
all three turn again
to the job at hand

there's work to be done
knees braced feet steadied
each cut coaxed
toward a merciful conclusion
the saw's whine lifting through trees
the sky accidentally still blue

therapy

something therapeutic
prying nails
grabbing a hammer
smacking an old wall down

busting a window frame
tossing out flooring
in heaps on the lawn

swinging that hammer
like an ax
splintering studs
ripping ten-penny toenails

driving to the landfill
heaping pickup loads
of crap

torching the rest of it
tending a bonfire
beside the highway

your private grievances
flaming openly

and all those strangers
speeding past

self-talk

thatched roadhouse cafe
high on a mountain pass
looking over the island

a dark-eyed waitress
tells me there's a busload
of contrary spirits
inside each of us

bitter adversaries
negotiating
a tentative ceasefire
near the furious edge

i'm sitting cliff-side
listening
to a din of screeching monkeys
in treetops beneath us
fogged over

this quarreling she says
goes on and on
insults and name-calling
threats and lies

neighbors

more than once i winched her car
back on the pavement
where she'd slid in the ditch

twice or three times
answered her call
to thaw frozen pipes

helped a delivery boy
heave a new fridge
up her back stairs

waved maybe in passing
but that's all there was
between us i think

and now that she's gone
unaccountably i miss
smoke rising from her chimney

and the one high window lit
i could view through the trees
in the darkened hillside yonder

first friday of the new year

still at the office
should be headed home

but sit transfixed
staring out the window

snow falling falling
slow flake by flake

relentless pace
this mounding

no shelter
how the years drift

how the tock tock tock
piles up against us

turns our hair white
buries us all

every day

he pedaled his rusted bike
same route
through town

old man in a wool coat
tattered hat
with earflaps
folded some days above his ears
some days not

old-style balloon tires
saddle seat
his arms spanning the handle grips
as if wrestling
a longhorn steer

his spine erect
gaze squared forward
his knees rising and falling

his routine
a marker of sorts for the rest of us
driving past

our deadlines and destinations
his progress
like the hands of a clock

the sun climbing the sky
shadows lengthening
everyday comforts
how we come to depend on them

every day
he pedaled and we passed him
then one day

not

he’s not well

our father insists
he’ll be okay
he’ll get better
everything works out
don’t worry

he’s worried
afraid of doctors
the way they probe
examine microscopically
scribble clipboard charts
pronounce without looking up
the word cancer

my sister calls to alert me
says she wasn’t supposed to tell
says not to worry
everything works out
says dad said it’ll be okay

i hear a little earthquake
in her voice

how ‘bout you
i ask
will you be okay

she chokes back a long silence
snuffles
clears her throat

he’s sick
she says
call him

at a matinee

spied one of my students
at a matinee
where i'd brought grandkids
he'd brought his son

i waved
he nodded
sheepishly i thought
because he'd missed class that morning
maybe worried
i'd judge him for that

he's a single dad
and works
enrolled in college
aiming to improve his lot

and he bolted with the kid in tow
as quick as the finale
though i'd hoped to speak
say there's more important things
than a degree
and i'd award him a gold star

for sitting with his boy
this afternoon sharing
slapstick nonsense
of a goofy cartoon

and nothing matters but the memories
popcorn and a fistful of laughter
and it's all over
so soon

listening

a pebble caught in my shoe
troubles my progress
halts me on a precipice
along a well-worn path overlooking the surf

i sit in tall grass
undo laces
lift the pebble
between my thumb and forefinger

ask what it has to say
solitary inaudible squeak
lost in the grand mashing
of tides pounding the shoreline

and did i mention
today is my sixtieth birthday
three score orbits
on a big rock in the black empty

well not such a big rock really
a pebble
in comparison to our daystar
even less to larger lights in the night sky

i pocket this quiet stone home
and sit with it in my palm late tonight
listening
to the winds pummeling the dunes
and the relentless ocean grinding

scaffolding

in the photo
i'm kneeling on planks

replacing a window

the photo snapped
from inside the house
so that what you see
is the outside me posed
in an empty window frame

as if i can float
in the shifting skies
drifting in from across the lake
and beyond

what you don't see
beneath my knees
is scaffolding
climbing two stories up
from decking below

i'd rented the scaffolding
pieced it together
twisting the wingnuts
till my thumbs bled
securing cross supports

there's a little wobble
as i work
and smile for the camera
wave for the camera bravely

i'm not afraid
i'm always afraid
there's a little wobble

but it holds

driving the back road home

the afternoon sun breaks
after weeks of grey

two horses play
in a hillside meadow

like children splash
in mud-green breezes

i pull over to watch
let golden rays relax my face

melt the overcast
i've carried with me

all this
important nonsense

blindingly simple
suddenly

while the horses snort
bob their heads

break right feint left
shudder prance preen

Lowell Jaeger is a graduate of the Iowa Writers' Workshop, winner of the Grolier Poetry Peace Prize, and recipient of fellowships from the National Endowment for the Arts and the Montana Arts Council. He has taught creative writing at Flathead Valley Community College (Kalispell, Montana) for the past 30 years, and he has also been self-employed for many years as a silversmith/goldsmith. In 2010, Jaeger was awarded the Montana Governor's Humanities Award for his work in promoting civil civic discourse.

Also by Lowell Jaeger:

How Quickly What's Passing Goes Past (Grayson Books, 2013)

New Poets of the American West (Many Voices Press, 2010)

WE (Main Street Rag Publishing, 2010)

Suddenly Out of a Long Sleep (Arctos Press, 2009)

Poems Across the Big Sky (Many Voices Press, 2007)

Hope Against Hope (Utah State University Press, 1990)

War On War (Utah State University Press, 1988)